MOSES AND THE LAWS OF GOD

a story from The Bible retold by MOLLY COX
illustrated by GRAHAM McCALLUM
from the BBC TV series *In The Beginning*

COLLINS ST JAMES'S PLACE LONDON

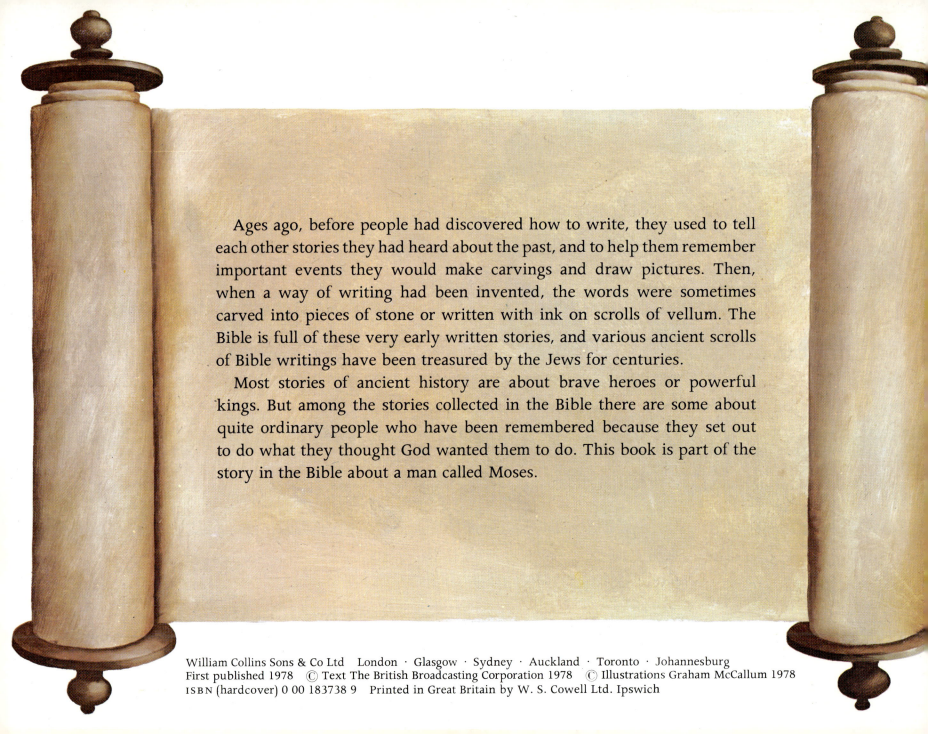

Ages ago, before people had discovered how to write, they used to tell each other stories they had heard about the past, and to help them remember important events they would make carvings and draw pictures. Then, when a way of writing had been invented, the words were sometimes carved into pieces of stone or written with ink on scrolls of vellum. The Bible is full of these very early written stories, and various ancient scrolls of Bible writings have been treasured by the Jews for centuries.

Most stories of ancient history are about brave heroes or powerful kings. But among the stories collected in the Bible there are some about quite ordinary people who have been remembered because they set out to do what they thought God wanted them to do. This book is part of the story in the Bible about a man called Moses.

William Collins Sons & Co Ltd   London · Glasgow · Sydney · Auckland · Toronto · Johannesburg
First published 1978   © Text The British Broadcasting Corporation 1978   © Illustrations Graham McCallum 1978
ISBN (hardcover) 0 00 183738 9   Printed in Great Britain by W. S. Cowell Ltd. Ipswich

At one time the first minister of the great King of Egypt was a foreigner – Joseph, the Jew. During his life his family and many other Jewish families came from Canaan to Egypt to live and work. When Joseph was old he called all his fellow countrymen together and said to them: "The day will come when God will bring you out of this land of Egypt and take you back to the land of your fathers, the land he gave to Abraham, Isaac and Jacob." And then he died.

As the years passed, the people of Egypt forgot that Joseph had done good things for them. When the new King, the next Pharaoh, came to power he noticed how many Jewish families had come to Egypt to settle, and he was afraid of them. So he ordered that they were to be treated as slaves, to work in his fields and build his great cities.

But still the Jewish tribes continued to grow in numbers. Then Pharaoh made another decree. Every boy born to a Jewish family was to be thrown in the river Nile to die. But one baby boy was rescued, and he was rescued by Pharaoh's own daughter. She heard the baby crying when she went down to the river to bathe. So she had him brought up in her own house and gave him the name Moses and taught him all the wisdom of Egypt.

When he was grown up, Moses left Egypt and went to live in the hills and worked as a shepherd. One day when he was with his sheep near the holy mountain of Horeb, he noticed a strange bush that seemed to be alive with fire. Then from out of the flames a voice called him by name.

"Here I am," said Moses and went towards the bush, but the voice said, "Come no nearer. You stand on holy ground. I am the God of your fathers." Moses was afraid to look and covered his face.

Then the voice said: "The time has come to save my people from their suffering. You are to go back to Egypt to Pharaoh, the King, and tell him

to let the Jews go home. And then you are to lead them across the desert to the land I once gave their fathers."

And Moses said: "O my Lord, send someone else on this errand. I am not an eloquent man and I will never be able to persuade Pharaoh with my clumsy words; and the Jews, what if they will not listen to me either? What if they say, 'Who is this God who has spoken to you?' What should I say to them?"

And the Lord God said, "Say to the Jews, 'The God of Abraham, God of Isaac, God of Jacob sent me.' I am the God who is. I shall be with you, they will listen to you."

So Moses went back into Egypt to do what God had told him to do. He went to the families of the Jews and told them what the Lord God had said, and they believed him. Then, he went in front of Pharaoh, the King of Egypt, and said: "I am sent here to you by the God of the Jews. He has said, tell Pharaoh to let my people go out of this land into the wilderness, so that they can worship me on the holy mountain."

"I do not know this God," said Pharaoh, "I will not let them go."

And he gave orders that the Jewish workers were to be beaten even more cruelly so that they would not listen to what Moses had to say.

And the Lord said to Moses, "I am their God and I will save them. Go again to Pharaoh, and this time I will work signs and wonders so that all Egypt will know that I am the Lord God."

The next morning Moses went to wait for Pharaoh by the banks of the river, and when he saw him coming he lifted up his staff, and all at once all the rivers of Egypt and the waters of the great river Nile itself turned into blood. But still Pharaoh would not listen to Moses.

Then Moses stretched out his arms to heaven, and God sent down thunder and lightning and hail: such a terrible storm as had never been seen in Egypt before or since. At last Pharaoh said, "Ask your God to stop it, and your people can go." But after the storm had stopped, Pharaoh changed his mind.

This time Moses said, "The Lord God of the Jews says: 'Let my people go, or behold, a plague of locusts will cover this land and eat every growing thing on it.'"

Then Pharaoh's servants turned to him and said, "Egypt will be ruined. You must let them go." And Pharaoh said to Moses, "How many of your people wish to go?" And Moses said, "All the people of God." Then Pharaoh was angry and shouted, "All of you! No! Never!"

So Moses stretched out his staff again, and an east wind blew and a dense swarm of locusts came and settled over the country, till the ground

was black with them. They ate every plant and every green and living thing on it. But still Pharaoh would not let the Jews go.

Then Moses raised his hand towards heaven and a thick darkness came down and covered the land. "There will be great sorrow in Egypt," said Moses. "This night, an Angel of the Lord will pass through the midst of you and the eldest child of each family will die. From the child of Pharaoh's family to the child of the miller's daughter." And Pharaoh said, "Get out of my sight. If ever I see you again, you shall die." And Moses said, "As you say, Pharaoh, King of Egypt, I will not see you again."

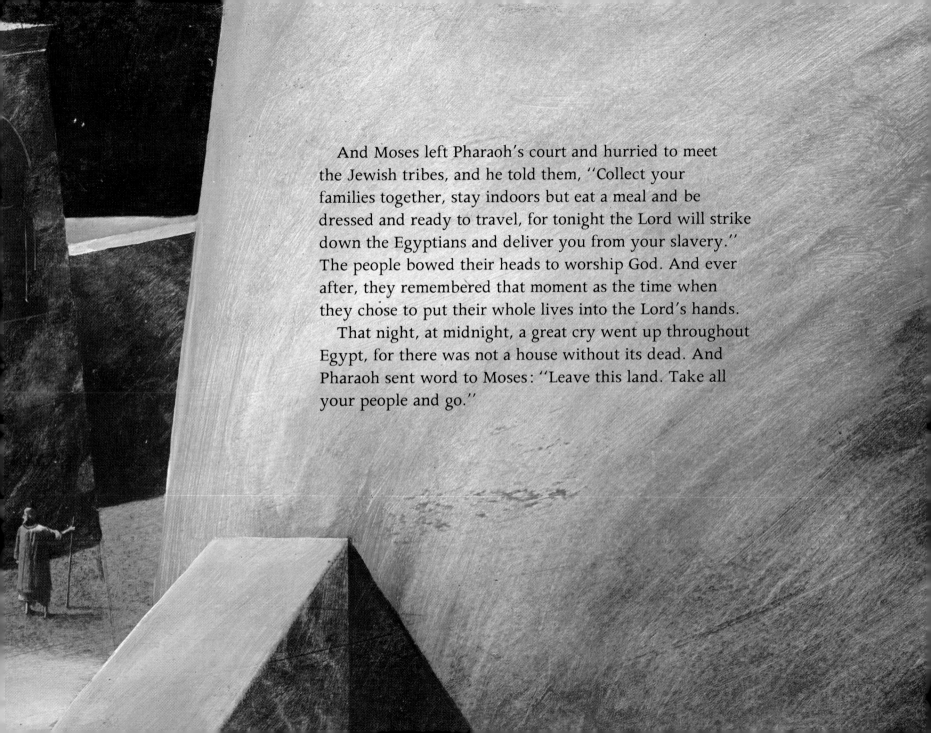

And Moses left Pharaoh's court and hurried to meet
the Jewish tribes, and he told them, "Collect your
families together, stay indoors but eat a meal and be
dressed and ready to travel, for tonight the Lord will strike
down the Egyptians and deliver you from your slavery."
The people bowed their heads to worship God. And ever
after, they remembered that moment as the time when
they chose to put their whole lives into the Lord's hands.

That night, at midnight, a great cry went up throughout
Egypt, for there was not a house without its dead. And
Pharaoh sent word to Moses: "Leave this land. Take all
your people and go."

So the people of God, hundreds of them, left Egypt, taking with them the bones of Joseph, their ancestor. And God went before them in a cloud. They marched all night and all day until they reached the shores of the sea.

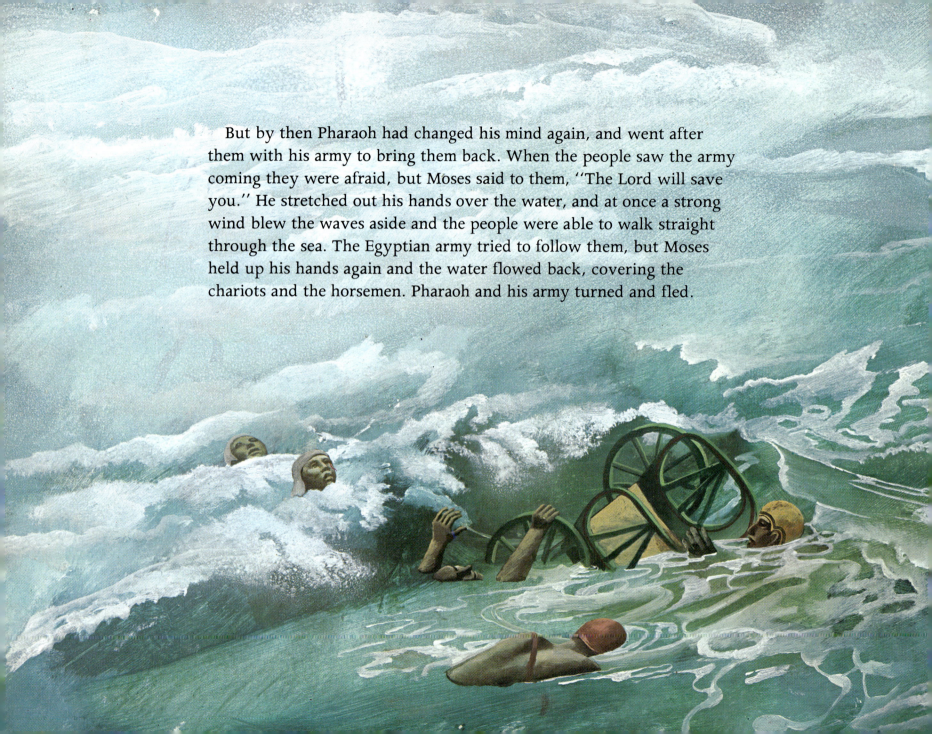

But by then Pharaoh had changed his mind again, and went after them with his army to bring them back. When the people saw the army coming they were afraid, but Moses said to them, "The Lord will save you." He stretched out his hands over the water, and at once a strong wind blew the waves aside and the people were able to walk straight through the sea. The Egyptian army tried to follow them, but Moses held up his hands again and the water flowed back, covering the chariots and the horsemen. Pharaoh and his army turned and fled.

The Jews were astonished by the power of the Lord God and of his servant Moses. They followed Moses out into the wild desert towards the land of Canaan where their fathers had once lived. But in the desert there was no water and no food, and the people turned on Moses and said, ''When we were in Egypt we were slaves, but we ate bread. Here we will starve and our children will die.'' And as they were complaining, they looked out towards the wilderness, and there in a cloud shone the glory of the Lord, and a voice spoke:

''So that you will learn that I am the Lord your God, I will make bread rain from heaven for you.'' And the next morning the ground was covered with a white powder, like frost. ''It is the bread God gives you to eat,'' said Moses. ''Each morning he will provide more.'' So the people ate the bread from heaven – which they called Manna – and it tasted like wafers mixed with honey.

Some time later they arrived in the desert of Sinai, and there Moses took them to the mountain where God was. As they came near, a trumpet sounded, the ground shook and the mountain seemed to be on fire. Then a loud voice spoke from the mountain and the people trembled.

"I am your God, the Lord Almighty.
Love me and keep my laws.
You are to serve no other God.
Keep one day in the week holy – in my name.
Respect your father and your mother.
Do not murder.
Do not steal.
Do not seduce another man's wife.
Do not deceive others.
Do not envy others for what they possess."

The voice was so loud that the people were terrified and cried out to Moses: "If we hear the voice of the Living God again, we shall die. You go to him and listen and then come back and tell us what it is he wants."

So Moses went alone towards the darkness and the flames. When he came back he repeated to the people the laws that God had given them. And the people answered with one voice: "We will do all that God asks." And God called to Moses: "Come up to the top of the mountain and I will write down my laws for you." So Moses climbed up to where God's glory was.

And God said, "Tell the people to make a shrine, and in this shrine keep these slabs of stone on which I have written for you the rules of life. Keep the shrine in a tent, and there I will come to meet you. You are my friend and I will always be with you."

Then Moses asked God, "Allow me, now, to see your face." And God said, "No man can look at me and live. But I will let my splendour pass near you, and as I pass I will put out my hand to shield your eyes." So Moses went and hid in a cleft in the rocks, and when the glory of God passed before him, he cried out, "O Lord God, maker of all things, you are indeed a God of tenderness and forgiveness." And he worshipped him; and Moses remained there on the mountain for forty days.

Then he left God and went down the mountain carrying in his arms the two slabs of stone on which God's own hand had written. But as he came near to the tents of his people, he heard shouts and chanting, and the sounds of dancing. He saw an image of a bull calf made of gold, which was set up on an altar, and the people were offering sacrifices to it, as if it were a God.

Moses was so angry that he threw down the stone slabs and broke them, and he shouted out, "Whoever is for the Lord God of the Jews, come with me!" And the people were ashamed, and they broke the bull statue into pieces and threw them into the fire.

So Moses went again to the mountain, and God wrote the words of his commands a second time; and when Moses returned, his face shone with a light so bright that people could not look at him. Then Moses told them to make the shrine in which to keep God's written commands. It was to be made out of wood and precious gold, and around it they made a tent from blue and violet and scarlet stuff, rich with embroidery. They would never make an image of God, for God Almighty did not show his face to any man, but in front of the shrine they put a lamp with seven branches.

Moses went into the tent, and there he spoke to God as if he were a friend. And he chose some of the people to be priests of the Lord. They looked after the tent and carried the shrine before the people as they set off again on their journey.

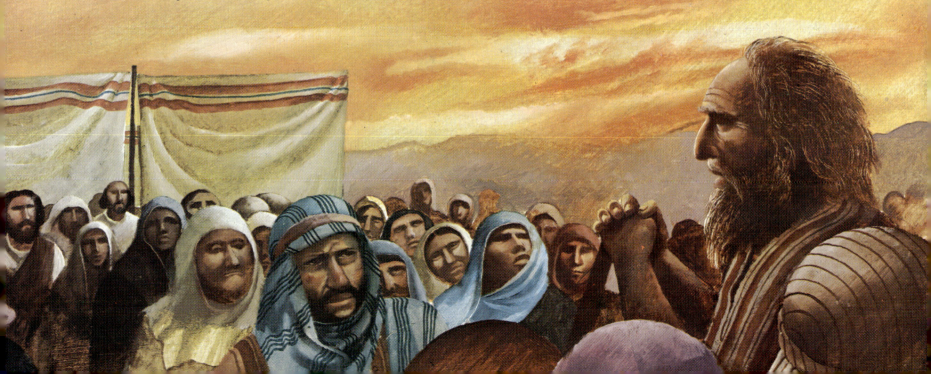

For forty years Moses led the tribes through the wilderness, telling them again and again of the laws of God, until at last they came in sight of the river Jordan and the land of their fathers.

Then Moses called them all together and said, "I am an old man now and I will die before you reach the Promised Land. So now I will remind you again of the agreement God has made with you. The Lord has made you a people set apart, not because you are greater than other nations – indeed you are the smallest – but because he loves you. The land ahead is to be your home, and you, for your part, must love God and follow his ways. It is not too hard a task for you to do. The laws of God are not strange secrets to be brought back from a distant land, or mysteries to spend a lifetime seeking. You have them with you always, printed on your memory, written in your heart. Live by them.

"And God has promised that out of this nation will come another leader, a new prophet. When he comes listen to him."

And there, in front of all the people, before he died, Moses prayed:

"There is no one as great as the Lord your God,
The clouds themselves make way for his splendour,
As he rides through the heavens to come to your help.
Your resting place is in the eternity of God,
And always his arms reach out to hold you up."